Commerce

&

Advertising Management

:: Author ::

Pareshkumar M. Thakor

PUBLISHED BY

Hemchandracharya International Publishing House
HQ. At & Po. Chaveli., Ta- Chansma,
Dist- Patan, North Gujarat, India, Asia.
www.iphouseindia.com

First Publication: 5th April, 2015

Copyright: Author

(c) **Pareshkumar M. Thakor**

ISBN:- 978-15-12032-20-8

Price: Rs.750/- INDIA

$ 15 OUTSIDE INDIA

PUBLISHED BY

Hemchandracharya International Publishing House
HQ. At & Po. Chaveli., Ta- Chansma,
Dist- Patan, North Gujarat, India, Asia.
www.iphouseindia.com

Advertising Management

Advertising simply put is telling and selling the product. **Advertising Management though is a complex process of employing various media to sell a product or service.** This process begins quite early from the marketing research and encompasses the media campaigns that help sell the product. Without an effective advertising management process in place, the media campaigns are not that fruitful and the whole marketing process goes for a toss. Hence, companies that believe in an effective advertising management process are always a step ahead in terms of selling their goods and services.

As mentioned above, advertising management begins from the market research phase. At this point, the data produced by marketing research is used to identify what types of advertising would be adequate for the specific product. Gone are the days when there was only print and television advertising was available to the manufacturers. These days apart from print and television, radio, mobile, and Internet are also available as advertising media. Advertising management process in fact helps in defining the outline of the media campaign and in deciding which type of advertising would be used before the launch of the product.

If you wish to make the advertising effective, always remember to include it from the market research time. Market research will help to identify the niche segment of the population to which the product or service has to be targeted from a large population. It will also identify why the niche segment would opt for the product or service. This information will serve as a guideline for the preparation of advertising campaigns.

Once the niche segments are identified and the determination of what types of advertising will be used is done, then the advertising management focuses on creating the specifics for the overall advertising campaign. If it is a radio campaign, which type of ads would be used, if it is a print campaign, what write ups and ads will be used, and if it is a television campaign, what type of commercials will be used. There might also be a mix and match advertising in which radio might supplement television advertising and so on. It is important that through advertising management the image is conveyed that all the strategies complement each other. It should not look to public that the radio advertising is focusing on something else while television on something else. The whole process in the end should benefit the product or service.

The role of people designing the advertising campaign is crucial to its success. They have been trained by seasoned professionals who provide the training in the specific field. Designing an advertising campaign is no small a task and to understand the consumer behavior from the data collected from market research is a very important aspect of the campaign. A whole lot of creativity and inspiration is required to launch an adequate advertising campaign. In addition, the management skills come into play when the work has to be done keeping the big picture in mind. **It would be fruitful for the company if the advertising campaign lasts well over the lifetime of a product or service, reach the right customers, and generate the desired revenue.**

Classification of Advertising

Advertising is the promotion of a company's products and services though different mediums to increase the sales of the product and services. It works by making the customer aware of the product and by focusing on customer's need to buy the product. Globally, advertising has become an essential part of the corporate world. Therefore, companies allot a huge part of their revenues to the advertising budget. Advertising also serves to build a brand of the product which goes a long way to make effective sales.

There are several branches or types of advertising which can be used by the companies. Let us discuss them in detail.

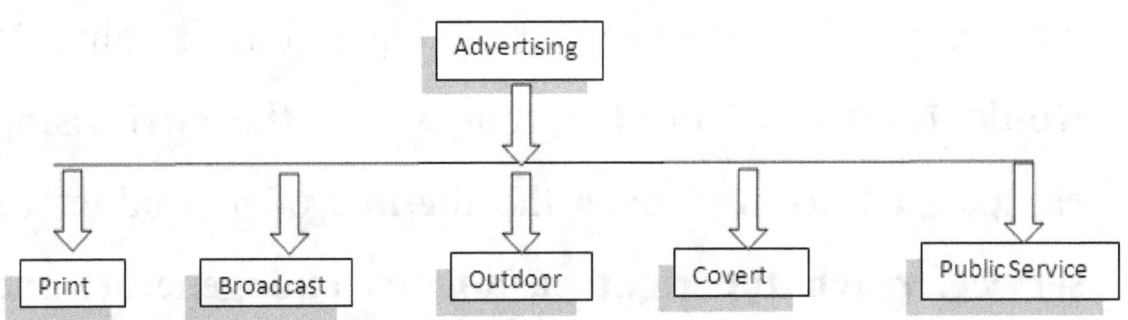

Classification of Advertising

1. <u>**Print Advertising**</u> - The print media has been used for advertising since long. The newspapers and

magazines are quite popular modes of advertising for different companies all over the world. Using the print media, the companies can also promote their products through brochures and fliers. The newspaper and magazines sell the advertising space and the cost depends on several factors. The quantity of space, the page of the publication, and the type of paper decide the cost of the advertisement. So an ad on the front page would be costlier than on inside pages. Similarly an ad in the glossy supplement of the paper would be more expensive than in a mediocre quality paper.

2. **Broadcast Advertising** - This type of advertising is very popular all around the world. It consists of television, radio, or Internet advertising. The ads on the television have a large audience and are very popular. The cost of the advertisement depends on the length of the ad and the time at which the ad would be appearing. For example, the prime time ads would be more costly than the regular ones. Radio advertising is not what it used to be after the advent of television and Internet, but still there is specific audience for the

radio ads too. The radio jingles are quite popular in sections of society and help to sell the products.

3. **<u>Outdoor Advertising</u>** - Outdoor advertising makes use of different tools to gain customer's attention. The billboards, kiosks, and events and tradeshows are an effective way to convey the message of the company. The billboards are present all around the city but the content should be such that it attracts the attention of the customer. The kiosks are an easy outlet of the products and serve as information outlets for the people too. Organizing events such as trade fairs and exhibitions for promotion of the product or service also in a way advertises the product. Therefore, outdoor advertising is an effective advertising tool.

4. **<u>Covert Advertising</u>** - This is a unique way of advertising in which the product or the message is subtly included in a movie or TV serial. There is no actual ad, just the mention of the product in the movie. For example, Tom Cruise used the Nokia phone in the movie Minority Report.

5. **<u>Public Service Advertising</u>** - As evident from the title itself, such advertising is for the public causes. There are a host of important matters such as AIDS, political integrity, energy conservation, illiteracy, poverty and so on all of which need more awareness as far as general public is concerned. This type of advertising has gained much importance in recent times and is an effective tool to convey the message.

Print Advertising

Print advertising is a widely used form of advertising. **These advertisements appear in newspapers or magazines and are sometimes included as brochures or fliers**. Anything written in the print media to grab the attention of the specific target audience comes under the purview of print advertising.

People who read newspapers or other publications have a tendency to browse the print ads that they come across. The decision to buy the product might not be instantaneous, but it does settle down in their subconscious mind. Next time they see the product in the market, they are tempted to buy it.

Print advertisements are only effective when people see them. When people browse through newspapers and publications, these advertisements should grab the attention of the potential customer. Therefore, these advertisements should be created in such a manner that they can hold the attention of the customer to some extent. Usually a team of individuals is required in order to design the advertisements.

The newspaper or magazine ad should be such that it should compel people to spend money on the products. This is just what the advertising team does. To create such an ad, the team members work on a concept and develop the wordings and images of the ad. These wordings and images are then brought together to form the final ad. Then there are people who deal with the placement of the ad. They have to make sure that if the client has paid for premium place, they get the desired exposure. For example, an ad on the first page will get instant attention of the reader than the ad on the subsequent pages. Likewise, an ad which occupies greater space is likely to get more attention. All these factors have to be looked into while designing the ad.

The sales team of the publication makes sure that it gets ads regularly. In fact, these ads are a major source of income for the publication and hence it is expected that there should be a constant flow of the ads. The sales team does just that.

Mailers are another type of print ads. These can range from well-designed postcards to simple paper leaflets. These are usually delivered by the postal workers in people's mailboxes. The problem with these mailers is that they get least attention and are usually considered as junk and thrown away even without reading. To reduce this occurrence, companies sometimes make use of fliers. These are paper ads which are handed over to individuals in person. The logic is that if the ad is given to people personally, they will pay more attention to it, which is actually true to some extent.

Though print advertising is still very popular, it does take a hit from time to time. For example, during the recession phase, when people's budgets were tight, they did not resort to print ads. In addition, with the advent of Internet, the print ads in the publications have gone down because Internet has a wider reach online. To overcome this scenario, new strategies have to be developed by advertisers and the print media. Globally, advertisers keep on developing strategies which benefit the business of print publications. Therefore, it can be said that print advertising is here to stay.

Broadcast Advertising

Generally speaking, **broadcast advertising is radio, television, and Internet advertising**. The commercials aired on radio and televisions are an essential part of broadcast advertising.

The broadcast media like radio and television reaches a wider audience as opposed to the print media. The radio and television commercials fall under the category of mass marketing as the national as well as global audience can be reached through it.

The role of broadcast advertising is to persuade consumers about the benefits of the product. It is considered as a very effective medium of advertising. The cost of advertising on this channel depends on the time of the commercial and the specific time at which it is aired. For example, the cost of an ad in the premium slot will be greater than in any other slot.

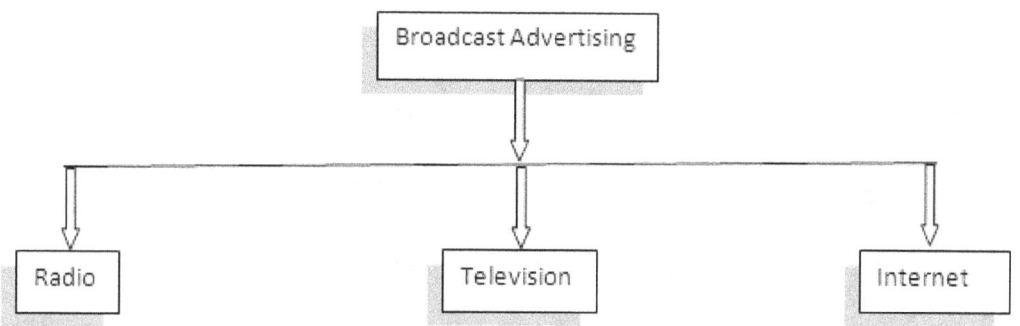

A **radio ad** must be aired several times before it actually sinks in the minds of the consumers. Thus the frequency of the ad is important. The type of your target audience is also important. Therefore, one must do a research on which type of audience listens to which channels if they want the ads to be successful. The voice talent in the commercial should be taken keeping in mind the type of audience and the type of commercial.

The **television advertising** is usually considered the advertising for the corporate giant, though even the small businesses can benefit from it. A strong audio and video combination is a must for the success of the commercial. But it is also important that the audio and video should function well without each other. For example, if a person is not viewing the TV but just listening to it, s/he should get the idea and vice versa.

It is extremely important that whatever has been advertised in the commercial is true. For this reason, organizations such as Federal Trade Commission (FTC) are there to monitor the commercials on television and radio. This ensures that the advertisers are not making any false claims to lure consumers to buy their products.

Most of the radio and television advertisements are paid though there are some public service ads which can be aired for free. The advertisers usually have to pay for the spot which lasts for 30 seconds. In rare cases, this spot can increase to 60 seconds too.

These days radio and television ads are prepared by advertising agencies for their clients. They understand the need of the client and make the commercial keeping in mind the current state of affairs. Broadcast advertising has become a very essential part of marketing in recent times. Companies allocate specific budget for radio and television ads and make an estimate of how much revenue they can earn through broadcast advertising. For example, marketing consultants are hired to determine the return on investment (ROI) for spending on radio and television ads. Sometimes the marketing consultants of these businesses run sample ads to judge its popularity among the viewers.

Internet or online advertising uses the Internet or the World Wide Web for the purpose of attracting consumers to buy their product and services. Examples of such advertising include ads on search engine result pages, rich media ads, banner ads, social network advertising, and email marketing and so on. Online advertising has its benefits, one of them being immediate publishing of the commercial and the availability of the commercial to a global audience. But along with the benefits come the disadvantages too. These days, advertisers put distracting flashing banners or send across email spam messages to the people on a mass scale. This can annoy the consumers and even the real ads might get ignored in the process. Therefore, ethics in advertising is very important for it to be successful.

Whatever the mode of advertising, broadcast advertising is an inherent part of any advertising campaign these days.

Outdoor Advertising

Outdoor advertising communicates the message to the general public through highway billboards, transit posters and so on. **Outdoor advertising is a very important form of advertising as the ads are huge and are visible to one and all**. The important part of the advertising is that the message to be delivered should be crisp and to the point. Though images can be used, but they cannot be used in excess. Everything should be presented to the viewer in such a format so that the viewers make up their mind to buy the product or service.

The message to be delivered can be an ad to buy a product, take a trip, vote for a politician, or give to a charity. According to Outdoor Advertising Association of America (OAAA), millions of dollars are being spent on outdoor advertising each year and the figures are expected to grow. This is due to the fact that outdoor traffic keeps on growing every year and hence the target audience for outdoor advertising is ever increasing.

The print and newspaper advertising takes up a huge part of advertising but outdoor advertising is unique in its own way. It is an extremely cost-effective method of advertising. All you need to do is to design a billboard and get it printed as compared to the television advertising where an entire 30 second commercial has to be designed. If the outdoor ads are strategically placed, it can guarantee substantial exposure for very little cost. That is why outdoor advertising is very cost-effective.

Different industries make use of outdoor advertising in their own different way. For example, eating joints and eateries on the highway make use of highway billboards to draw the customer to have a bite and rest a little at their joint. Mac Donalds and Subway are the excellent examples. The automobile and tourism industries make use of the billboards to advertise their products and tourism plans. These are way too successful because of the fact that people on the highway are on the lookout for such information.

Apart from the billboards, there are several other forms in which outdoor advertising can take place. For example, beverage companies make use of sporting events and arenas to showcase their products. For example, Coca Cola was one of the FIFA World Cup sponsors. Other places where you can see outdoor advertising are:

- taxicabs
- buses
- railways
- subways and walls on which murals are painted

All these forms of outdoor advertising are very popular and extremely cost effective.

The OAAA has divided the Outdoor Advertising into four major categories: **Billboards** - These usually account for almost half of the revenue of outdoor advertising. Then there is **transit system and mobile advertising** which also takes up a major pie of outdoor advertising. **Advertising on public furniture** is also used comprehensively these days globally. Last but not the least is **alternative advertising**. Such advertising can be in the form of Corporate blogging which is an important form of advertising these days.

To conclude, one can say that outdoor advertising, if used wisely is very powerful and cost-effective way of advertising.

Covert and Public Service Advertising

As evident from the word "covert", **this type of advertising aims to integrate the advertising with the non-promotional mediums**. This practice is most-commonly found in films. For example, billboards of the products may be shown in the film for a prolonged period of time. Or a character in the film may mention the name of the brand again and again. At other times the director may present the product as an integral part of the film. For example, the cars featured in several action flicks. Remember the Cadillac in Matrix Reloaded and BMWs in James Bond movies.

It is a fact that these tactics seem to be high profile and also seem to require a lot of bucks. Only established brand names have used such form of advertising. Not everyone has the financial prowess to use this form of advertising. However, there are ways through which you can also promote your product or service. May be contributing an article in local daily will work well for you. You can mention your brand quite subtly there. On the Internet too, covert advertising is a hot trend. You can blog about the product or ask a well-known blogger to write about your product or service. However, this should be done inconspicuously.

As opposed to covert advertising, **public service advertising aims at spreading awareness about issues that are relevant to public interest**. Such ads may quote a political viewpoint, a philosophy, or a religious concept. Such humanitarian ads are usually broadcasted on the radio or television, though they can also appear in newspapers and magazines. A PSA or Public Service Announcement is aimed to alter public attitudes on issues ranging from health, safety, and conservation.

Most of the PSA ads use celebrities in order to gain attention. Others focus their ads on the risks that can come to men, women, and children. In recent years, it has become quite common in US to broadcast the public service ads just after or in between the programs that relate to public service in any way. They provide information such as the toll free help lines, websites and addresses. In general, the public service ads are about rape, HIV, cancer, child abuse, domestic violence, and civil rights.

While public service advertising is not as popular as paid advertising, it should be given due importance. All across the world, such type of advertising is now widely used. In fact, in US, public service advertising was once a requirement if the radio and television stations were to get their licenses from Federal Communications Commission (FCC).

Public Service Advertising should carry a short and to the point message. The advertisement should be made keeping the target audience in mind. As it is not about buying a product but a change in the attitude altogether, the advertisements have to be amply clear and the message should prompt the people to take a step forward. If the shift in the mindsets of people does not happen, then the ad is not conveying the message properly. For this reason, the PSA's are often dramatic and expressive.

Objectives and Importance of Advertising

Advertising is the best way to communicate to the customers. Advertising helps informs the customers about the brands available in the market and the variety of products useful to them. Advertising is for everybody including kids, young and old. It is done using various media types, with different techniques and methods most suited.

Let us take a look on the main objectives and importance of advertising.

Objectives of Advertising

Four main Objectives of advertising are:

  i.   Trial
  ii. Continuity
  iii. Brand switch
  iv. Switching back

Let's take a look on these various types of objectives.

1. **Trial:** the companies which are in their introduction stage generally work for this objective. The trial objective is the one which involves convincing the customers to buy the new product introduced in the

market. Here, the advertisers use flashy and attractive ads to make customers take a look on the products and purchase for trials.

2. **Continuity:** this objective is concerned about keeping the existing customers to stick on to the product. The advertisers here generally keep on bringing something new in the product and the advertisement so that the existing customers keep buying their products.

3. **Brand switch:** this objective is basically for those companies who want to attract the customers of the competitors. Here, the advertisers try to convince the customers to switch from the existing brand they are using to their product.

4. **Switching back:** this objective is for the companies who want their previous customers back, who have switched to their competitors. The advertisers use different ways to attract the customers back like discount sale, new advertise, some reworking done on packaging, etc.

Basically, advertising is a very artistic way of communicating with the customers. The main characteristics one should have to get on their objectives are great communication skills and very good convincing power.

Importance of Advertising

Advertising plays a very important role in today's age of competition. Advertising is one thing which has become a necessity for everybody in today's day to day life, be it the producer, the traders, or the customer. Advertising is an important part. Lets have a look on how and where is advertising important:

1. **Advertising is important for the customers**

   Just imagine television or a newspaper or a radio channel without an advertisement! No, no one can any day imagine this. Advertising plays a very important role in customers life. Customers are the people who buy the product only after they are made aware of the products available in the market. If the product is not advertised, no customer will come to know what products are available and will not buy the product even if the product was for their benefit. One more thing is that advertising helps people find the best products for themselves, their kids, and their family. When they come to know about the range of products, they are able to compare the products and buy so that they get what they desire after spending their valuable money. Thus, advertising is important for the customers.

2. **Advertising is important for the seller and companies producing the products**

Yes, advertising plays very important role for the producers and the sellers of the products, because

- Advertising helps increasing sales
- Advertising helps producers or the companies to know their competitors and plan accordingly to meet up the level of competition.
- If any company wants to introduce or launch a new product in the market, advertising will make a ground for the product. Advertising helps making people aware of the new product so that the consumers come and try the product.

- Advertising helps creating goodwill for the company and gains customer loyalty after reaching a mature age.

- The demand for the product keeps on coming with the help of advertising and demand and supply become a never ending process.

3. **Advertising is important for the society**

Advertising helps educating people. There are some social issues also which advertising deals with like child labour, liquor consumption, girl child killing, smoking, family planning education, etc. thus, advertising plays a very important role in society.

Marketing Communications - Meaning and its Process

Marketing communications is essentially a part of the marketing mix. The marketing mix defines the 4Ps of marketing and Promotion is what marketing communications is all about. It is the message your organization is going to convey to your market. You need to be very particular about different messages you are going to convey through different mediums.

Traditionally printed marketing was the whole sole method of conveying the messages to the consumers. However, in recent times, emails, sms, blogs, television and company websites have become the trendy way of conveying the organization's message to the consumers. It is important though that the message you give in one medium should tally with the message provided in other medium. For example, you should use the same logo in on your website as the one you use in your email messages. Similarly, your television messages should convey the same message as your blogs and websites.

For the above reason, people controlling the marketing communication process are very important for the company. These executives make it an integrated marketing communication process. You would now understand why it has to be 'integrated'. The reason is that the messages to be conveyed through different mediums should be the same.

Let us now look at the marketing communication process. It is very important to have a process in place because then your advertising will reap proper benefits. There is an old advertising joke "I know my advertising works, I don't know which half." That's why if the marketing communication process puts a tab on advertising because companies cannot bear to lose dollars on wrong type of advertising. Things have to be well-defined and integrated to get maximum revenues. **Your marketing communication process would look like:**

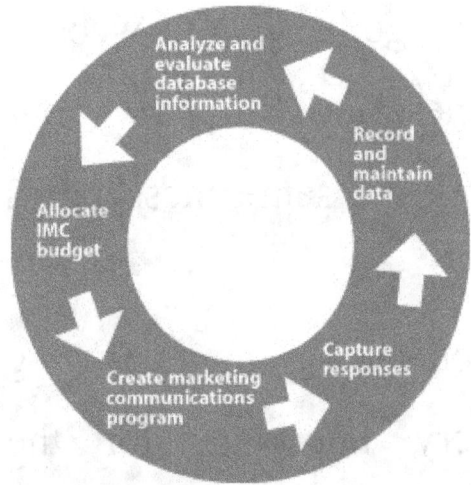

The **marketing communication process identifies where the investments are being done and what is bringing more return on investment**. Therefore, you can alter the advertising campaign to reap maximum benefits.

The process begins at the strategic development stage. You start by creating a marketing communications program. At this point, you decide what all will fall in your advertising bracket. At the next stage, you capture responses of your consumers. These responses are then recorded and maintained as advertising data. The executives then analyze and evaluate the collected data. They generate the all important reports which will help to allocate the integrated marketing and communications budget.

The integrated marketing communications is a data-driven approach which identifies the consumer insights and develops a strategy with the right combination of offline and online channels which should result in a stronger brand-consumer relationship. It has grown manifolds in recent years due to several shifts in the advertising and media industry. This is the reason why it has developed into a primary strategy for the developers. Some examples of shifts are from media advertising to the multiple forms of communication, from general focus advertising to data based marketing and so on.

Selecting the most important communications elements is crucial for the success of company's business. The advertising campaign should be effective across all platforms. Once the integrated marketing process is set, the company can reap rich dividends from it. These days, there are companies that specialize in creating the marketing communications process for you. So you can either do it on your own or take their services. But an effective marketing communication process is the order of the day!

Consumer Communication and Persuasion

Consumer communication and persuasion is an essential part of any Marketing Strategy. In fact, it is the starting point of all improvement as consumer voices provide companies with the data such as where they are lacking and what all they could do to improve the product or service.

Do all companies listen to the consumer voices? Not really. It is only the ones which have an effective consumer communication process in place, that are really able to focus on consumer needs. Are you one of them? Let us take a look at the consumer communication process at Suntory to understand the Consumer Communication Process.

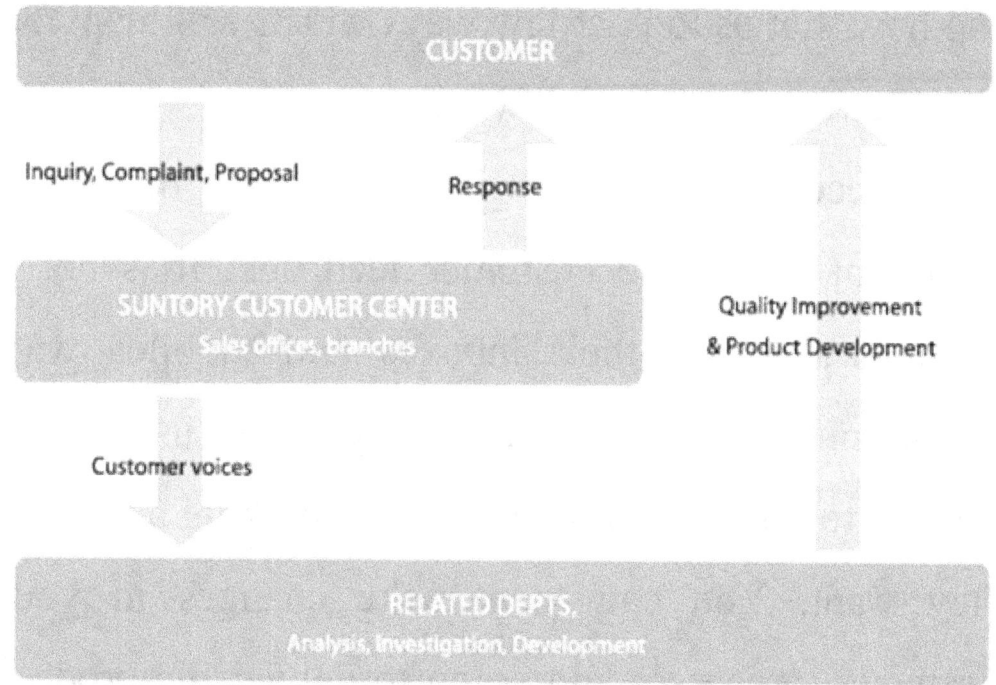

This company has set up a Customer Centre which takes up all inquiries, complaints, and proposals from customers. Though most of the queries are answered, the customer voices are sent across to related departments of the company. These departments analyze the gap between the customer needs and the products and services. After doing so, the quality improvements are suggested and the product development takes place in keeping with the customer demands.

Consumer communication should be used effectively to drive maximum benefits to the company. You must be thinking how. Let us look at few ways which will help you market effectively even in a downturn.

1. When economy is changing, it is all the more important to get the customer feedback. It is not a good idea to fill their inboxes and mobiles with promotional messages. More so, you can use online surveys to understand how they are thinking and what they want. You can then make changes in your strategies, processes and so on to deliver the product that your consumers are aiming for.

2. It is just not important to feed information to your consumers. Having a dialogue with them from time to time is also important. You can use the email marketing newsletters to invite them for such conversations. Apart from understanding their concerns, showing your consumers that you care is also very important. This will have far-reaching consequence and will benefit your company's image.

3. Try and co-host an event with another local business. This will highlight your product's image in a positive manner. This is a kind of customer relationship

building activity where you interact face-to-face with the consumer and show him your expertise.

4. Consumers are becoming more and more environmentally aware these days. Anything against the environment would put you in a bad light. So focus that your product or service is following all the environment friendly standards. You can also show your concern by teaming up with local charity and involving your consumers in the event too.

The above points can also be used for consumer persuasion too. Face-to-face meetings are more effective in persuading people to buy your stuff. People can judge easily whether what you are saying has substance or not. Therefore, try your level best to portray the positive image of your product in a positive fashion. Once you learn the essence of consumer communication, you would never have to look back.

Consumer Behaviour - Meaning, Determinants and its Importance

Companies make investment in understanding consumer behaviour and implementing strategies, which will help them retain customers.

Consumers can be categorized as an individual consumer and organizational/industrial consumers. Understanding their behaviour and buying pattern is important in ultimate survival of companies in the market place.

Consumer behaviour consists of activities/process followed in making any buying decision of goods as well as a service. In recent time service (holiday, travel, etc.), decisions are forming large part of consumer behaviour.

One thing needs to be highlighted here is that consumer behaviour does not end with purchase of goods or service, but also post purchase activities are included in consumer behaviour.

Consumer behaviour and consumption behaviour are two different concepts developed and cannot be used as a substitute. Consumer behaviour deals with the process of an individual or organization in coming to the purchase decision, whereas consumption behaviour is a study focus on consuming unit or service.

Furthermore, there is a difference between consumer behaviour and buying behaviour. Consumer behaviour as highlighted before talks about process and actions taken by the final or end users where as buyer behaviour looks at intermediate users (who add value to goods and service) and final users.

Understanding of the consumer behaviour begins with study of the consumer buying process. Consumer buying process is five step activities. The starting with **need recognition**, which leads to **information search**, once information is obtained from different sources next step, is the **evaluation and intent** where in consumer evaluates various parameters of the product or service. The next step in five-step activity is **the purchase decision** where in intent is converted into an actual purchase of the good or the service. The final step is **post-purchase reaction** where in customer if she is satisfied with goods or services recommends to other prospective customers or repeat the purchase. If the customer is not happy with purchase, a bad word of mouth follows, and she looks for alternative product or service.

Three factors are identified as determinants to consumer behaviour namely economic determinants, psychological determinant and sociological determinant. Economic Determinants are personal income (individual's purchasing power), family income (total purchasing power of the family), the future income expectations (expected increase or decrease in availability of disposable income), availability of liquid asset (asset, which can be converted to cash), consumer market credit (if market conditions are good credit easily available) and social class (effluent class, upper-middle class, middle class, etc.).

In compare the industrial buying process is much more formal process done according to pre-defined policy and norms. The key features of organization buying are it's a formal and standardized process, it is done in large quantities and may be done at periodic intervals of time, and decision-making process usually involves more than one individual.

As there are determinants for consumer behaviour, similar industrial buying behaviour has its own set of determinants, which are overall objectives of the organization, technological capabilities of the organization which consist of information systems and network capabilities and finally organization structure, which includes its capital and number of employees.

From above it can be comprehended that **consumer behaviour is important factor in determining marketing policies**.

Media Strategy in Advertising

Every work to be done needs a plan of action so that the work is done in a desired and correct manner. Media Strategy plays a very important role in Advertising. The role of Media Strategy is to find out the right path to transfer or say deliver the message to the targeted customers.

How many people see or hear or read all the advertisements or promotional offers and buy the product or service? The basic intention of media strategy is not only procuring customers for their product but also placing a right message to the right people on the right time and of course that message should be persuasive and relevant. So, here the planners of the organization decide the Media Strategy to be used but keeping the budget always in mind. The Media Strategy process has three "**W**"s to be decided. They are

- **Where to advertise ?**
- **When to advertise ?**
- **What media type to use ?**

Where is the place for showing or delivering advertisement. In short it means the geographical area from where it should be visible to the customers who use or are most likely to use the product or services offered. The place does not mean only TV or radio but it can also be newspapers, blogs, sponsorships, hoardings on roads, ads in the movie break in theatres, etc. The area varies from place to place like it can be on national basis, state basis and for local brands it can be on city basis.

When is the timing to show or run advertisement. For e.g. you cannot show a raincoat ad in the winter season but you need to telecast ad as soon as the summer season is coming to an end and rainy season is just about to begin. The ad should be delivered with perfect timing when most customers are like to buy the product. The planners need to plan it keeping the budget in mind as the maximum of 20% of revenues of the company can be used in the advertisement section. Different products have different time length for advertisements. Some products need year long ads as they have nothing to do with seasonal variations e.g. small things like biscuits, soaps, pens, etc and big services like vehicle insurance, refrigerators, etc. Some products need for three or four months. E.g. umbrellas, cold creams, etc. So the planners have to plan the budget according to the time length so that there is no short of money at any time in this process.

What is what type of media is to be used for delivering the message.

There are basically two media approaches to choose from.

- Media Concentration approach
- Media Dispersion Approach

In media concentration approach, the number of categories of media is less. The money is spent on concentrating on only few media types say two or three. This approach is generally used for those companies who are not very confident and have to share the place with the other competitors. They don't want anyone to get confused with there brand name so this is the safest approach as the message reaches the target consumers.

In media dispersion approach, there are more number of categories of media used to advertise. This approach is considered and practiced by only those people who know that a single or two types of media will not reach their target. They place their product ads in many categories like TV, radio, internet, distributing pamphlets, sending messages to mobiles, etc.

Selection of Media Category

Whichever category is selected by the planners of the organization, they should select a proper media to convey their message.

If the product is for a big amount of customers then a mass media option can be selected like TV, radio or newspaper. The best examples for this type are detergent ads, children health drinks and major regular used products such as soap, shampoo, toothpastes etc.

If the planners want to change the mind of people doing window shopping or just doing shopping for sake of name, then point of purchase type can be opted by the company. This helps the company to explain their point to the buyers and convince the buyers to go for their product.

If the planners want to sell their product on one to one basis, then the third option is direct response type. Here, the company people directly contact the customers via emails, text messages, phone calls or meeting for giving demos. The best example of this type of media is the Life cell Cord Blood Banking. They go to their customers, explain them what it is all about and try to convince them.

Thus, this process of media strategy plays an important and vital role in the field of Advertising.

Advertising Agencies - Meaning, its Role and Types of Agencies

"The work of a tailor is to collect the raw material, find matching threads, cut the cloth in desired shape, finally stitch the cloth and deliver it to the customer."

Advertising Agency is just like a tailor. It creates the ads, plans how, when and where it should be delivered and hands it over to the client. Advertising agencies are mostly not dependent on any organizations.

These agencies take all the efforts for selling the product of the clients. They have a group of people expert in their particular fields, thus helping the companies or organizations to reach their target customer in an easy and simple way.

The first Advertising Agency was William Taylor in 1786 followed by James "Jem" White in 1800 in London and Reynell & Son in 1812.

Role of Advertising Agencies

1. Creating an advertise on the basis of information gathered about product

2. Doing research on the company and the product and reactions of the customers.

3. Planning for type of media to be used, when and where to be used, and for how much time to be used.

4. Taking the feedbacks from the clients as well as the customers and then deciding the further line of action

All companies can do this work by themselves. They can make ads, print or advertise them on televisions or other media places; they can manage the accounts also. Then why do they need advertising agencies? The reasons behind hiring the advertising agencies by the companies are:

- The agencies are expert in this field. They have a team of different people for different functions like copywriters, art directors, planners, etc.

- The agencies make optimum use of these people, their experience and their knowledge.

- They work with an objective and are very professionals.

- Hiring them leads in saving the costs up to some extent.

There are basically **5 types of advertising agencies**.

1. Full service Agencies

- Large size agencies.
- Deals with all stages of advertisement.
- Different expert people for different departments.

- Starts work from gathering data and analyzing and ends on payment of bills to the media people.

2. Interactive Agencies

- Modernized modes of communication are used.
- Uses online advertisements, sending personal messages on mobile phones, etc.
- The ads produced are very interactive, having very new concepts, and very innovative.

3. Creative Boutiques

- Very creative and innovative ads.
- No other function is performed other than creating actual ads.
- Small sized agencies with their own copywriters, directors, and creative people.

4. Media Buying Agencies

- Buys place for advertise and sells it to the advertisers.
- Sells time in which advertisement will be placed.
- Schedules slots at different television channels and radio stations.

- Finally supervises or checks whether the ad has been telecasted at opted time and place or not.

5. In-House Agencies

- As good as the full service agencies.

- Big organization prefers these type of agencies which are in built and work only for them.

- These agencies work as per the requirements of the organizations.

There are some specialized agencies which work for some special advertisements. These types of agencies need people of special knowledge in that field. For example, advertisements showing social messages, finance advertisements, medicine related ads, etc.

Social and Economical Aspects of Advertising

"Every coin has two sides"

Advertising is praised but also criticized by critics in their own ways. Advertising has many positive impacts along with its negative pictures. As the President of American Association of Advertising Agencies, John O' Toole has described advertise is something else. It is not related to studies, but it educates. It is not a journalist but gives all information. And it is not an entertaining device but entertains everyone.

Now let's go through the economic and social aspects of advertising.

Economic role of Advertising

Value of Products:

The advertised products are not always the best products in the market. There are some unadvertised products also present which are good enough. But advertising helps increase value for the products by showing the positive image of the product which in turn helps convincing customers to buy it. Advertising educates consumers about the uses of the products hence increasing its value in minds of the consumers. For e.g. mobile phones were first considered as necessity but nowadays the cell phones come with number of features which makes them mode of convenience for consumers.

Effect on Prices:

Some advertised products do cost more than unadvertised products but the vice versa is also true. But if there is more competition in the market for those products, the prices have to come down, for e.g., canned juices from various brands. Thus some professional like chartered accountants and doctors are not allowed to advertise.

But some products do not advertise much, and they don't need much of it and even their prices are high but they are still the leaders in market as they have their brand name. e.g., Porsche cars

Effect on consumer demand and choices:

Even if the product is heavily advertised, it does not mean that the demand or say consumption rates will also increase. The product has to be different with better quality, and more variety than others. For E.g., Kellogg's cornflakes have variety of flavors with different ranges to offer for different age groups and now also for people who want to loose weight thus giving consumers different choices to select from.

Effect on business cycle:

Advertising no doubt helps in employing more number of people. It increases the pay rolls of people working in this field. It helps collecting more revenues for sellers which they use for betterment of product and services. But there are some bad effects of advertisements on business cycle also. Sometimes, consumer may find the foreign product better than going for the national brand. This will definitely effect the production which may in turn affect the GDP of the country.

The economic aspects are supported by the Abundance Principle which says producing more products and services than the consumption rate which helps firstly keeping consumers informed about the options they have and secondly helps sellers for playing in healthy and competitive atmosphere with their self interest.

Social role of Advertising:

There are some positive and some negative aspects of advertising on the social ground. They are as follows.

Deception in Advertising:

The relation between the buyers and sellers is maintained if the buyers are satisfied with what they saw in advertise and what they got after buying that product. If seller shows a false or deceptive image and an exaggerated image of the product in the advertisement, then the relation between the seller and buyers can't be healthy. These problems can be overcome if the seller keep their ads clean and displays right image of the product.

The Subliminal Advertising:

Capturing the Minds of the consumers is the main intention of these ads. The ads are made in such a way that the consumers don't even realizes that the ad has made an impact on their minds and this results in buying the product which they don't even need. But "All ads don't impress all consumers at all times", because majority of consumers buy products on basis of the price and needs.

Effect on Our Value System:

The advertisers use puffing tactics, endorsements from celebrities, and play emotionally, which makes ads so powerful that the consumers like helpless preys buy those products.

These ads make poor people buy products which they can't afford, people picking up bad habits like smoking and drinking, and buy products just because their favorite actor endorsed that product. This affects in increased the cost of whole society and loss of values of our own selves.

Offensiveness:

Some ads are so offensive that they are not acceptable by the buyers. For example, the ads of denim jeans showed girls wearing very less clothes and making a sex appeal. These kinds of ads are irrelevant to the actual product. Btu then there is some ads which are educative also and now accepted by people. Earlier ads giving information about birth control pills was considered offensive but now the same ads are considered educative and important.

But at the last, there are some great positive aspects which help

- Development of society and growth of technologies
- Employment
- Gives choices to buyers with self interest
- Welcomes healthy competition
- Improving standard of living.
- Give information on social, economical and health issues.

Steps in Advertising Process

"Mass demand has been created almost entirely through the development of Advertising"

Calvin Coolidge in the New York Public Library.

For the development of advertising and to get best results one need to follow the advertising process step by step.

The following are the **steps involved in the process of advertising:**

1. **Step 1 - Briefing:** the advertiser needs to brief about the product or the service which has to be advertised and doing the <u>SWOT analysis of the company and the product</u>.

2. **Step 2 - Knowing the Objective:** one should first know the objective or the purpose of advertising. i.e. what message is to be delivered to the audience?

3. **Step 3 - Research:** this step involves finding out the market behavior, knowing the competitors, what type of advertising they are using, what is the response of the consumers, availability of the resources needed in the process, etc.

4. **Step 4 - Target Audience:** the next step is to identify the target consumers most likely to buy the product. The target should be appropriately identified without any confusion. For e.g. if the product is a health drink

for growing kids, then the target customers will be the parents who are going to buy it and not the kids who are going to drink it.

5. **Step 5 - Media Selection:** now that the target audience is identified, one should select an appropriate media for advertising so that the customers who are to be informed about the product and are willing to buy are successfully reached.

6. **Step 6 - Setting the Budget:** then the advertising budget has to be planned so that there is no short of funds or excess of funds during the process of advertising and also there are no losses to the company.

7. **Step 7 - Designing and Creating the Ad:** first the design that is the outline of ad on papers is made by the copywriters of the agency, then the actual creation of ad is done with help of the art directors and the creative personnel of the agency.

8. **Step 8 - Perfection:** then the created ad is re-examined and the ad is redefined to make it perfect to enter the market.

9. **Step 9 - Place and Time of Ad:** the next step is to decide where and when the ad will be shown.

   The place will be decided according to the target customers where the ad is most visible clearly to them. The finalization of time on which the ad will be telecasted or shown on the selected media will be done by the traffic department of the agency.

10. **Step 10 - Execution:** finally the advertise is released with perfect creation, perfect placement and perfect timing in the market.

11. **Step 11 - Performance:** the last step is to judge the performance of the ad in terms of the response from the customers, whether they are satisfied with the ad and the product, did the ad reached all the targeted people, was the advertise capable enough to compete with the other players, etc. Every point is studied properly and changes are made, if any.

If these steps are followed properly then there has to be a successful beginning for the product in the market.

Advertising Techniques - 13 Most Common Techniques Used by the Advertisers

Today every company needs to advertise its product to inform the customers about the product, increase the sales, acquire market value, and gain reputation and name in the industry. Every business spends lot of money for advertising their products but the money spent will lead to success only when the best techniques of advertising are used for the product. So here are some very **common and most used techniques used by the advertisers to get desired results**.

1. Emotional Appeal

This technique of advertising is done with help of two factors - needs of consumers and fear factor. Most common appeals under need are:

- need for something new
- need for getting acceptance
- need for not being ignored
- need for change of old things
- need for security
- need to become attractive, etc.

Most common appeals under fear are:

- fear of accident
- fear of death
- fear of being avoided
- fear of getting sick
- fear of getting old, etc.

2. Promotional Advertising

This technique involves giving away samples of the product for free to the consumers. The items are offered in the trade fairs, promotional events, and ad campaigns in order to gain the attention of the customers.

3. Bandwagon Advertising

This type of technique involves convincing the customers to join the group of people who have bought this product and be on the winning side. For e.g. recent Pantene shampoo ad which says "15crores women trusted Pantene, and you?"

4. Facts and Statistics

Here, advertisers use numbers, proofs, and real examples to show how good their product works. For e.g. "Lizol floor cleaner cleans 99.99% germs" or "Colgate is recommended by 70% of the dentists of the world" or Eno - just 6 seconds.

5. Unfinished Ads

The advertisers here just play with words by saying that their product works better but don't answer how much more than the competitor. For e.g. Lays - no one can eat just one or Horlicks - more nutrition daily. The ads don't say who can eat more or how much more nutrition.

6. Weasel Words

In this technique, the advertisers don't say that they are the best from the rest, but don't also deny. E.g. Sunsilk Hairfall Solution - reduces hairfall. The ad doesn't say stops hairfall.

7. Endorsements

The advertisers use celebrities to advertise their products. The celebrities or star endorse the product by telling their own experiences with the product. Recently a diamond jewellery ad had superstar Amitabh Bacchan and his wife Jaya advertising the product. The ad showed how he impressed his wife by making a smart choice of buying this brand. Again, Sachin tendulkar, a cricket star, endorsed for a shoe brand.

8. Complementing the Customers

Here, the advertisers used punch lines which complement the consumers who buy their products. E.g. Revlon says "Because you are worth it."

9. Ideal Family and Ideal Kids

The advertisers using this technique show that the families or kids using their product are a happy go lucky family. The ad always has a neat and well furnished home, well mannered kids and the family is a simple and sweet kind of family. E.g. a dettol soap ad shows everyone in the family using that soap and so is always protected from germs. They show a florescent color line covering whole body of each family member when compared to other people who don't use this soap.

10.   Patriotic Advertisements

These ads show how one can support their country while he uses their product or service. For e. g some products together formed a union and claimed in their ad that if you buy any one of these products, you are going to help a child to go to school. One more cellular company ad had a celebrity showing that if the customers use this company's sim card, then they can help control population of the country.

11.　Questioning the Customers

The advertisers using this technique ask questions to the consumers to get response for their products. E.g. Amway advertisement keeps on asking questions like who has so many farms completely organic in nature, who gives the strength to climb up the stairs at the age of 70, who makes the kids grow in a proper and nutritious ways, is there anyone who is listening to these entire questions. And then at last the answer comes - "Amway : We are Listening."

12.　Bribe

This technique is used to bribe the customers with some thing extra if they buy the product using lines like "buy one shirt and get one free", or "be the member for the club for two years and get 20% off on all services."

13. **Surrogate Advertising**

This technique is generally used by the companies which cannot advertise their products directly. The advertisers use indirect advertisements to advertise their product so that the customers know about the actual product. The biggest example of this technique is liquor ads. These ads never show anyone drinking actual liquor and in place of that they are shown drinking some mineral water, soft drink or soda.

These are the major techniques used by the advertisers to advertise their product. There are some different techniques used for online advertising such as web banner advertising in which a banner is placed on web pages, content advertising using content to advertise the product online, link advertising giving links on different sites to directly visit the product website, etc.

Advertising Budget and Factors Affecting it

"Money does matter a lot."

Advertising Budget is the amount of money which can be or has to be spent on advertising of the product to promote it, reach the target consumers and make the sales chart go on the upper side and give reasonable profits to the company.

Before finalizing the advertising budget of an organization or a company, one has to take a look on the favorable and unfavorable market conditions which will have an impact on the advertising budget. The market conditions to watch out for are as follows:

- Frequency of the advertisement
- Competition and Clutter
- Market Share of the Product
- Product Life Cycle Stage

1. Frequency of the Advertisement

This means the number of times advertise has been shown with the description of the product or service, in the granted time slots. So here, if any company needs more advertising frequency for its product, then the company will have to increase its advertising budget.

2. Competition and Clutter

The companies may have many competitors for its product. And also there are plenty of advertisements shown which is called clutter. The company has to then increase their advertising budget.

3. Market Share

To get a good market share in comparison to their competitors, the company should have a better product in terms of quality, uniqueness, demand and catchy advertisements with resultant response of the customers. All this is possible if the advertisement budget is high.

4. Product Life Cycle Stage

If the company is a newcomer or if the product is on its introduction stage, then the company has to keep the budget high to make place in the market with the existing players and to have frequent advertisements. As the time goes on and product becomes older, the advertising budget can come down as then the product doesn't need frequent advertising.

When the market conditions are studied thoroughly, then the company has to set up its advertising budget accordingly. For setting advertising budget, there are four methods:

They are as follows.

- **Percentage Of Sales:** In this method, the budget is decided on the basis of the sales of the product from previous year records or from the predicted future sales. This is a pure prediction based method and best applicable to the companies which have fixed annual sales. But if in case there is a requirement for more promotional activities then this method has a disadvantage because there will be decrease in advertisements as the budget is fixed.

- **Affordability:** this method is generally used by the small companies. Only the companies which have funds and can afford advertising opt for this method. The companies can go for advertising at any time in whole year whenever they have money to spend. The amount spent also varies from time to time as per the advertisements takes place.

- **Best guess:** This method is basically for newcomers who have just entered the market and they have no knowledge or say they are not aware of how the market is and how much to spend on advertising. Thus, this method is applied by the higher level executives of the company as they are the only experienced people.

Thus, doing the homework and then moving forward, i.e. searching for best market conditions and setting the best advertising budget will have a great impact on improvement and development of the company.

Advertising Campaigns - Meaning and its Process

Advertising campaigns are the groups of advertising messages which are similar in nature. They share same messages and themes placed in different types of medias at some fixed times. The time frames of advertising campaigns are fixed and specifically defined.

The very prime thing before making an ad campaign is to know-

Why you are advertising and what are you advertising ?

Why refers to the objective of advertising campaign. The objective of an advertising campaign is to

- Inform people about your product
- Convince them to buy the product
- Make your product available to the customers

The **process of making an advertising campaign is as follows:**

1. **Research:** first step is to do a market research for the product to be advertised. One needs to find out the product demand, competitors, etc.

2. **Know the target audience:** one need to know who are going to buy the product and who should be targeted.

3. **Setting the budget:** the next step is to set the budget keeping in mind all the factors like media, presentations, paper works, etc which have a role in the process of advertising and the places where there is a need of funds.

4. **Deciding a proper theme:** the theme for the campaign has to be decided as in the colors to be

used, the graphics should be similar or almost similar in all ads, the music and the voices to be used, the designing of the ads, the way the message will be delivered, the language to be used, jingles, etc.

5. **Selection of media:** the media or number of Medias selected should be the one which will reach the target customers.

6. **Media scheduling:** the scheduling has to be done accurately so that the ad will be visible or be read or be audible to the targeted customers at the right time.

7. **Executing the campaign:** finally the campaign has to be executed and then the feedback has to be noted.

Mostly used media tools are print media and electronic media. Print media includes newspaper, magazines, pamphlets, banners, and hoardings. Electronic media includes radio, television, e-mails, sending message on mobiles, and telephonic advertising. The only point to remember is getting a proper frequency for the ad campaign so that the ad is visible and grasping time for customers is good enough.

All campaigns do not have fix duration. Some campaigns are seasonal and some run all year round. All campaigns differ in timings. Some advertising campaigns are media based, some are area based, some are product based, and some are objective based. It is seen that generally advertising campaigns run successfully, but in case if the purpose is not solved in any case, then the theory is redone, required changes are made using the experience, and the remaining campaign is carried forward.

Models of Advertising Scheduling

Scheduling directly refers to the patterns of time in which the advertisement is going to run. It helps fixing up the time slots according to the advertiser so that the message to be delivered will reach target audience in a proper way with proper timings. There are basically three models of advertising scheduling as follows:

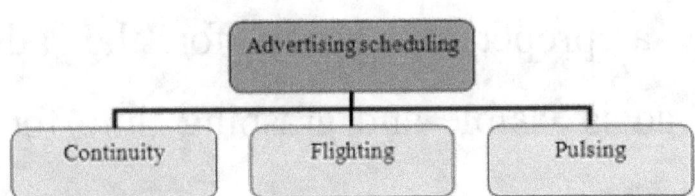

1. **Continuity:** This model is very good option for the products or services which don't depend on season for advertisements. They run ads whole year round. The advertisements under this type run at regular and fixed intervals. The main advantage here is reminding about your products to the customers continuously. This model helps maintain a continuous and complete purchase cycle. This is a best model for the products having continuous demand all the year round. There can be a Rising Continuity in which some specific products are been advertised in the peak seasons for e.g. floaters are advertised more in rainy season while some products fall under a Falling Continuity in which either ads for new products are run or if there is any other change in the existing product. E.g. packaging of Pediasure, a kid's health drink is recently changed.

2. **Flighting:** This model is also called bursting. As the name suggests, this an absolute season based products model. The ads here run at very irregular intervals. Advertisements are for very shorter periods and

sometimes no ads at all. The ads are in concentrated forms. So, the biggest advantage here is there is very less waste of funds as the ads run only at the peak time when the product demand is on high. Television and radio are the most used media types in this method. So the advertisers who cannot afford the year long ads, this is a best option. E.g. ads for warm clothes in Indian Market.

3. **Pulsing:** This model is the combination of both continuity and flighting scheduling. Here, ads run whole year round but at a lower sidxe that means less ads, and heavy advertisements are preferred at the peak time. So this model has advantages of both the other models. Generally scheduling is fixed for a month. There are six types of scheduling method here.

- Steady pulse has fixed schedule for 12 months.
- Seasonal pulse has bunches of ads season wise.
- Period pulse regular basis ads.
- Erratic pulse refers to irregular ads normally used for changing old patterns.

- Start up pulse is used for new product with heavy advertisements.

- Promotional pulse refers to short period single use ads used basically for promoting products or events.

Using this interface, you can set the time periods in which you want to run your campaign. Then click OK button.

Thus, points to remember while scheduling an advertisement are:

- Selecting a proper media type for running ads

- Selecting a correct time for running ads so that the purpose is solved.

- Advertisements should be sufficient enough (in number) to deliver the message to the target.

Industrial Advertising - Business to Business Advertising

The most popular terminology used for industrial advertising is Business to Business advertising. This type of advertising generally includes a company advertising its products or services for the companies which actually uses same or similar products or services or we can say that the advertising company should produce the products which the other company needs for its productions or functions. For e.g. some mineral water companies which work on a smaller scale outsource the packaging bottles, the caps for bottles, the cover with name printed on it, etc. so for this, the advertisements of the manufacturers of bottles, caps and outer packaging paper can work.

A smaller to smaller and largest of all, every company has to do industrial advertising. For e.g. if a company is making coffee powder, it will sell its powder to the distributors who in turn will sale it to the retailers and wholesalers and also to the big companies who has a coffee machine for their employees. Thus companies manufacturing any products can be advertised to the other companies, like raw materials, the machineries used by other companies, spare parts of the machines which makes it work, anything.

Role of Industrial Advertising

- It minimizes the hunt for buyers.
- It helps in increasing sales of the company.

- It helps in making more and more distribution channels.

- It makes company work more efficiently to produce the desired product or service.

- It creates awareness among the customers or other companies about the products and services.

Process of Industrial Advertising

The strategies used in industrial advertising differ from company to company, as different companies have different products to be advertised. So, a single rule cannot work for all the companies' advertisements. But the basic process which can lead to a successful advertisement is: knowing the objective for advertising - identifying the target companies - researching about the market conditions and the competitors - creating the ad to be delivered - selecting media to be used - what should be the budget allotted - execution of the advertisement - getting the feedbacks from the customers.

Media types in Industrial Advertising

The media generally used in the industrial advertising is print media and direct marketing.

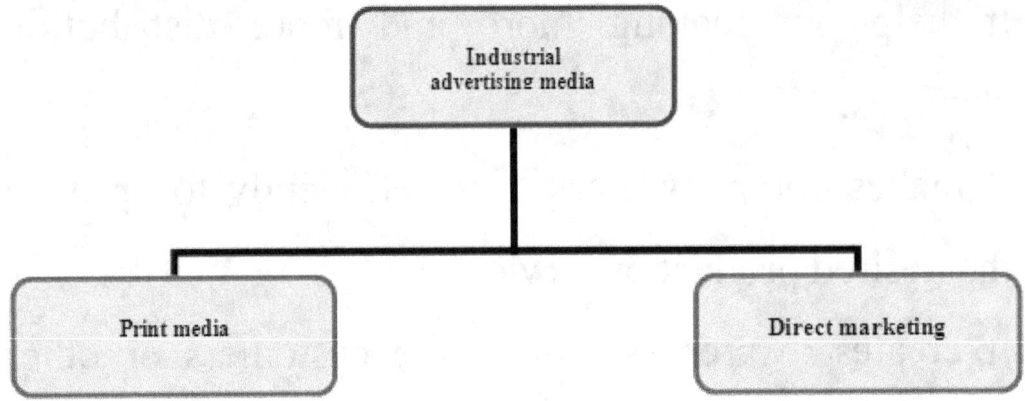

Print Media includes business magazines, trade publications, newspapers, technical journals, etc. To make print media work efficiently, there are some do's and don'ts to be kept in mind:

- Visual image of the ad should be very sharp and prominent
- The ad should be so impressive that readers get attracted towards reading it
- The highlight should be on the service or product offered and not the source by which it is being offered
- Let the ad be simple to be read (with no difficult fonts)
- The picture shown should not be irrelevant with the product.
- The ad should reflect the company's image.

- The ad should to be in logical sequence if it is of two or more pages.

- Headlines should be catchy and suiting the product image.

- And lastly, at the bottom of the page, the company name, address and phone number of the respected office should be mentioned clearly without fail.

Direct Marketing includes:

1. **Direct Mail -** here, the newsletters, data sheets, and the brochures of the company are directly mailed to the customers' postal address.

2. **Telephonic Advertising -** the advertising is done by calling up the customers on there telephones, giving messages on mobile phones, etc.

3. **Online Advertising -** includes companies sending e-mails to the customers or other companies enclosing information about their products ant services, putting online banners, providing e-shopping options, etc.

The advertisers also use other ways for promoting their products like participating in trade shows, trade expos, and fairs.

Thus, the companies can use any or every type of advertising, the important motto being increase in sales, producing best quality products, maintaining good relations with the customers, and achieving the desired goal.

Ethics in Advertising

Ethics means a set of moral principles which govern a person's behavior or how the activity is conducted. And advertising means a mode of communication between a seller and a buyer.

Thus ethics in advertising means a set of well defined principles which govern the ways of communication taking place between the seller and the buyer. Ethics is the most important feature of the advertising industry. Though there are many benefits of advertising but then there are some points which don't match the ethical norms of advertising.

An ethical ad is the one which doesn't lie, doesn't make fake or false claims and is in the limit of decency.

Nowadays, ads are more exaggerated and a lot of puffing is used. It seems like the advertisers lack knowledge of ethical norms and principles. They just don't understand and are unable to decide what is correct and what is wrong. The main area of interest for advertisers is to increase their sales, gain more and more customers, and increase the demand for the product by presenting a well decorated, puffed and colorful ad. They claim that their product is the best, having unique qualities than the competitors, more cost effective, and more beneficial. But most of these ads are found to be false, misleading customers and unethical. The best example of these types of ads is the one which shows evening snacks for the kids, they use coloring and gluing to make the product look glossy and attractive to the consumers who are watching the ads on television and convince them to buy the product without giving a second thought.

Ethics in Advertising is directly related to the purpose of advertising and the nature of advertising. Sometimes exaggerating the ad becomes necessary to prove the benefit of the product. For e.g. a sanitary napkin ad which shows that when the napkin was dropped in a river by some girls, the napkin soaked whole water of the river.

Thus, the purpose of advertising was only to inform women about the product quality. Obviously, every woman knows that this cannot practically happen but the ad was accepted. This doesn't show that the ad was unethical.

Ethics also depends on what we believe. If the advertisers make the ads on the belief that the customers will understand, persuade them to think, and then act on their ads, then this will lead to positive results and the ad may not be called unethical. But at the same time, if advertisers believe that they can fool their customers by showing any impractical things like just clicking fingers will make your home or office fully furnished or just buying a lottery ticket will make you a millionaire, then this is not going to work out for them and will be called as unethical.

Recently, the Vetican issued an article which says ads should follow three moral principles - Truthfulness, Social Responsibility and Upholding Human Dignity.

Generally, big companies never lie as they have to prove their points to various ad regulating bodies. Truth is always said but not completely. Sometimes its better not to reveal the whole truth in the ad but at times truth has to be shown for betterment.

Pharmaceutical Advertising - they help creating awareness, but one catchy point here is that the advertisers show what the medicine can cure but never talk about the side effects of that same thing or the risks involved in intake of it.

Children - children are the major sellers of the ads and the product. They have the power to convince the buyers. But when advertisers are using children in their ad, they should remember not to show them alone doing there work on their own like brushing teeth, playing with toys, or infants holding their own milk bottles as everyone knows that no one will leave their kids unattended while doing all these activities. So showing parents also involved in all activities or things being advertised will be more logical.

Alcohol - till today, there hasn't come any liquor ad which shows anyone drinking the original liquor. They use mineral water and sodas in their advertisements with their brand name. These types of ads are called surrogate ads. These type of ads are totally unethical when liquor ads are totally banned. Even if there are no advertisements for alcohol, people will continue drinking.

Cigarettes and Tobacco - these products should be never advertised as consumption of these things is directly and badly responsible for cancer and other severe health issues. These as are already banned in countries like India, Norway, Thailand, Finland and Singapore.

Ads for social causes - these types of ads are ethical and are accepted by the people. But ads like condoms and contraceptive pills should be limited, as these are sometimes unethical, and are more likely to loose morality and decency at places where there is no educational knowledge about all these products.

Looking at all these above mentioned points, advertisers should start taking responsibility of self regulating their ads by:

- design self regulatory codes in their companies including ethical norms, truth, decency, and legal points
- keep tracking the activities and remove ads which don't fulfill the codes.

- Inform the consumers about the self regulatory codes of the company

- Pay attention on the complaints coming from consumers about the product ads.

- Maintain transparency throughout the company and system.

When all the above points are implemented, they will result in:

- making the company answerable for all its activities

- will reduce the chances of getting pointed out by the critics or any regulatory body.

- will help gain confidence of the customers, make them trust the company and their products.

Measuring Advertising Effectiveness

"When a child writes the examination papers, he has to see the result come what it may be, so that he comes to know where he is wrong and where he should pay more attendance. This will help him work better in future."

This is exactly the case of the advertisement. The work is not complete if the effectiveness of advertise is not measured. This is the only way to know how the advertisement is performing, is it reaching the targets and is the goal achieved.

It is not at all possible to measure advertisement effectiveness accurately as there are many factors like making a brand image, increasing the sales, keeping people informed about the product, introducing new product, etc, which affect the effectiveness of an advertisement.

We all know that there are some companies who advertise at very low level but still their products are a hit and some companies indulge in very heavy advertisements but they don't get desirable results. But then, there are some traditional and modern tools to measure most of the effectiveness of an advertisement through which the advertiser can or may get more and more information about how their ads and product are performing in the market. According to Philip Kotler and Armstrong, the Gurus Of Marketing, there are two most popular areas which need to be measured for knowing the effectiveness of advertisement and they are:

- Communication Effect

· Sales Effect

Communication Effect Research consists of three types of researches:

1. **Direct Rating Method** - here, customers are directly asked to rate the advertisement and then these rating are calculated.

2. **Portfolio Tests -** here, the customers see the ads and listen carefully to the ads and all the contents of the ads and then they are asked to recall the ad and the contents. Then the calculations are done with help of this data.

3. **Laboratory tests -** here, the apparatus to measure the heart rates, blood pressure, perspiration, etc are used on the customer after he watches the ad, to know the physiological reactions of the body.

Sales Effect Research totally depends on the sales of the company. The sales keep varying from time to time. There are some factors affecting sales like product availability, the price of the product, contents of the product, and sometimes the competitors. So this method is a little difficult than the communication one. The company doing sales effect research generally bothers about the sales of the product, they try to know whether or not the money they are spending on the ads is enough or excess.

As earlier said, it is not possible to measure each and everything and the chances are at the lower end if the company has many ads running through various mediums at the same time. So suggestion is that the advertiser or the company should use appropriate and different methods which are most suitable for the media under use.

- The company can hold surveys and product recognition tests

- Questionnaire or feedback flyers can be distributed and customers could be asked to fill it up.

- Toll free number can be highlighted on the ads so that customers can call up.

- The response rates can be increased by telling customers what to do. For e.g. some ads have lines in flashy color like "Hurry Up" or "No one can eat just one" or "be the first" etc.

These are the traditional ways. Now days, internet is the modern tool for measuring the effectiveness of an advertisement. There are some types such as:

Integrated direct marketing - This is an internet based tool where they have a response corner designed on the websites. Whenever the customers visit the sites, they fill up their contact details and give feedbacks. Thus the company supplies more information and sends newsletters and also gets the idea for further action. But then its not that only online advertiser have this facility but then advertisers who don't work online can use coupons, discount vouchers, etc. to do this.

Analysis tool - there is an analysis tool available on internet by using which the advertiser will know how many customers are visiting the site, who are shopping online, how many pages are viewed, etc. which in turn will help advertiser to measure the effectiveness.

Internet is the most easy, cheaper and cost effective way to measure the effectiveness because here no money is wasted as the ad is only viewed when the customer want to view it where as in normal print method or using TV, the ad sometimes goes unwatched or unattended and viewed for the sake of viewing.

Advertising Myths - Ifs and Buts of the Advertising Industry

Advertising is considered as the best tool to make people aware of the product a company wants to sell. This is the best way to communicate with the audience and to inform them about the product but with a proper media selection and of course timing. But there are some myths which have been creating problems in the path of successful advertising. We have tried to **clarify some misinterpretations about the ifs and buts of the advertising industry**.

Advertising Myths

1. **Advertising works only for some business**

    Wrong. Advertising works for each and every company or business it only it is executed properly. But due to bad advertising, many ad campaigns fail to work in desired way and the people think that advertisements are not their cup of tea. They must understand one simple rule of advertising - it should be for right people at right time through right medium on right place.

2. Advertising is only needed when business is slow

Wrong. Who said that the big and successful brands don't advertise their products? Advertising is a continuous process with some renovations whenever needed. But, yes, when the business really is going slow or at its low, the advertising will have to be heavy and more in number. This will help the product to improve its market value and make people aware of the product.

3. If the product is not selling, advertise it

This is just not true. Just think about it. If you are selling a product which is not at all in vogue, and no one is using it, how will it get clear from the shelf. You need to understand the need of customers and then sell the product. Advertise doesn't mean selling anything you want but it means selling what customers wants.

4. Advertise creates needs

No. The people already had cassettes to play and listen to music they liked when they didn't have the option of CDs. It is technology which came in, and it was only then CDs were advertised and sold. Advertise only replaces the old things with new, it doesn't creates needs.

5. Advertise effects persist for decades

It's the quality of the product which persists. Advertise no doubt helps increasing sales of the product and stays in memory of the people, but minds are captured by the product itself.

6. Humuor in ads

Sometimes humour gets in the way of delivering message properly to the consumers but not every time it creates problems. Many of the times it helps people to remember the ad and the product and helps creating a positive attitude towards the advertise.

7. Sex sells

Not always. Some advertisers use sex for just increasing the sales and forget that the product doesn't need this type of ad at all. Remember once models

Milind Soman and Madhu Sapre posed naked for a shoe brand. It was really irrelevant.

8. Creativity is the most important factor

The ad should be no doubt creative enough to attract consumers but it not the only selling factor. There has to be good message to deliver, best media selection, and best quality of the product to make the product and ad both successful.

9. Advertising costs so much

Advertise needs money but one has to also consider the results in forms of increased sales, increased reputation in industry, recognition for product and also increased market value of product which advertisements brings along. Lets consider advertising as investment and not expense.

Thus these are the most common myths of the ad industry which are working as hurdles in the way of bright future of advertisers and advertising and we need to overcome these hurdles and rise.

Future of Advertising

Advertising is still all about the 'ifs and buts of a product', presented in a glowing rainbow like picture trying to attract consumers....but what is the future of advertising in coming years ?

Lets go way back when the idea of advertising a product was regarded as some kind of a big deal. Then the advertisements were very limited, and it took lots and lots of efforts to make a single advertisement. And the customers then, had no option other than watching those advertisements. Now, time has changed. Since last 20 years or lets just consider last 10 years, there has been a dramatic change in the world of advertisement. And this will not have a stopage in coming years. The change doesn't mean that the advertising agencies will all be shut down and firms will take over. It just means that the existing advertising agencies will have to experience a change in the industry and within. They will be redefined and reinvented so that they can survive in the years ahead. The agencies which gave their number of years to this industry will also change for good, be capable to cope up with new challenges, new competition and new attitudes of the consumers. Once a article was written on change in advertising in 1992 and the title then also suits now, it said - **Advertising Age : Change or Die** and very well said. To understand what is going to change and what will remain the same should be on the top of the list of the advertisers.

Now is the beginning of the digital era. The agencies had a system of having some few creative people who used to come with ideas for ads. That was the time when giving an ad in radio and television was very expensive. But now no one minds actually about the cost for such ads because consumers are responding well. But now and onwards, internet and technology has taken a front seat. Lets talk about the mass media. Today every tv serial, all movies running in theatres and all breaks in the radio channels have fillers called ads. But in the coming years, the ads can be shown to the consumers only if they want to see and not because the advertiser want them to see it. The cost of using internet and digital gadgets is everyday dropping down so the customers don't mind spending on these things other that fooling themselves with the colorful advertisements. The future will be in favour of the advertisers and advertisements but only at the cost of proper management and proper use of digital technologies and internet.

The Bond

Nowdays, no one trusts the ad industry because there is no transparency. The ethics are not being the part of ads anymore. In coming years, the bond of trust has to be again rebuilt between the consumers and the advertisers. The advertisers will have to work hard to gain the confidence of the customers.

More Creativity

The creative people of the agencies should not limit their creativity by only working with the old style menu. This is the time to explore with help of internet and digital tools.

Differentiated Products

The advertisers should launch a product which will be completely different but excellent to use. Then only the voice will be heard.

Attract Talent

More and more quality people should be hired today who will be leaders for tomorrow. They will be the people who will lead the industry in the future with the best quality being coping up will everything. Better HR practices should also be appointed.

These are some points which may help advertisers to survive and survive in a better way in the future. The people who will not change can just not stay in this new industry.

www.ingramcontent.com/pod-product-compliance
Lightning Source LLC
Chambersburg PA
CBHW080829180526

45168CB00006B/2621